A group of Methodists, in 1835, set up tents among a grove of oak trees. These tents were called "society tents", and were arranged in a semicircle on Trinity Park. The tents were cramped and set up dormitory style with men and women divided by a canvas center divider. Over time, families began to set up permanent structures. Soon congregations from all over came to meet here at Martha's Vineyard Camp Meeting. They would stay for a week of spiritual rejuvenation. This eventually lead to stores, hotels and larger homes being built to handle the increasing number of tourists to the area.

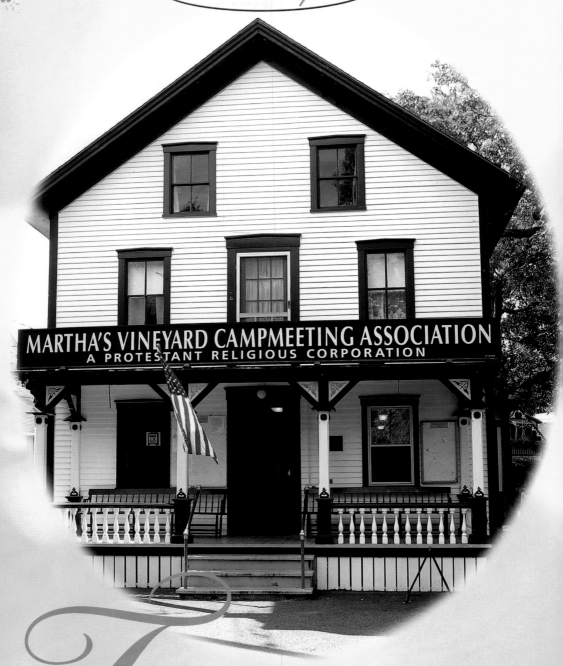

There is a cottage museum that is located just south of Trinity Park. You can see what the original cottages looked like from the inside as well as many artifacts from the past. On display you can find many vintage photographs, and other documents documenting the history of the campground. There is also a gift shop inside.

In the middle of Trinity Park you will find two structures. One is the Tabernacle, which is an open-air structure with beautiful stained glass. It was used for worship during the warmer months. The other structure is Trinity United Methodist Church. It was built in the mid 1800s for worship during the colder months. Currently it is used year around.

As the years passed, more and more returning campers started to build permanent cottages to replace the tents. They started to show more elaborate woodwork as time went by with the cupolas, spires, turrets, and even second and third stories added. The intricate trim and paint make the cottages feel like a you're in a magical wonderland.

THE
BISHOP GILBERT HAVEN
COTTAGE.
VISITED BY PRES. GRANT 1874

14

Aerial view of Campgrounds and Oak Bluffs Harbor.

The most noted features of the cottages are the porches with rocking chairs. Each cottage has a little different color or design in the porch. You may also notice that the intricate woodwork does not stop there. You will see specially designed screen doors, as well as trim along the rooflines and windows. You will also see the colorful flower boxes and hanging flower baskets. These flowers add even more color to the already beautiful cottages.

ELDER BERRY

Gazebo at Oak Bluffs Harbor.

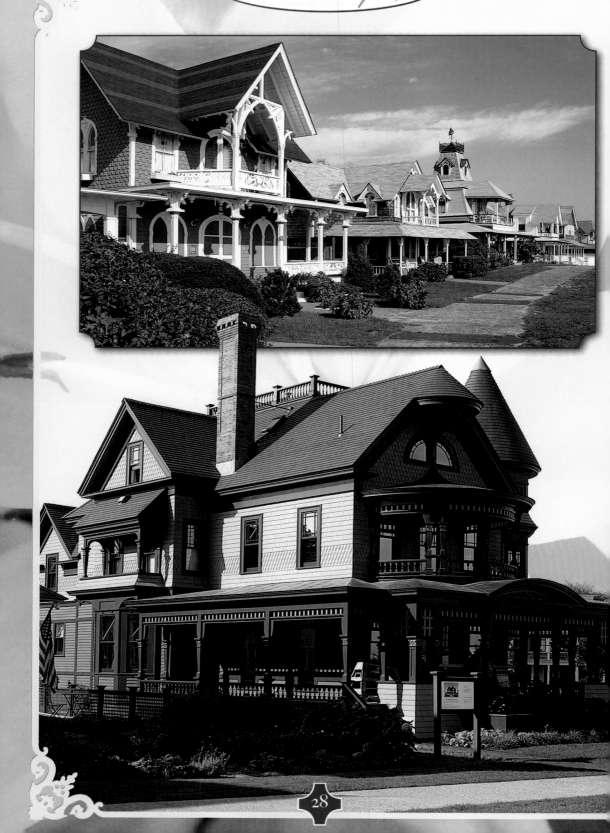

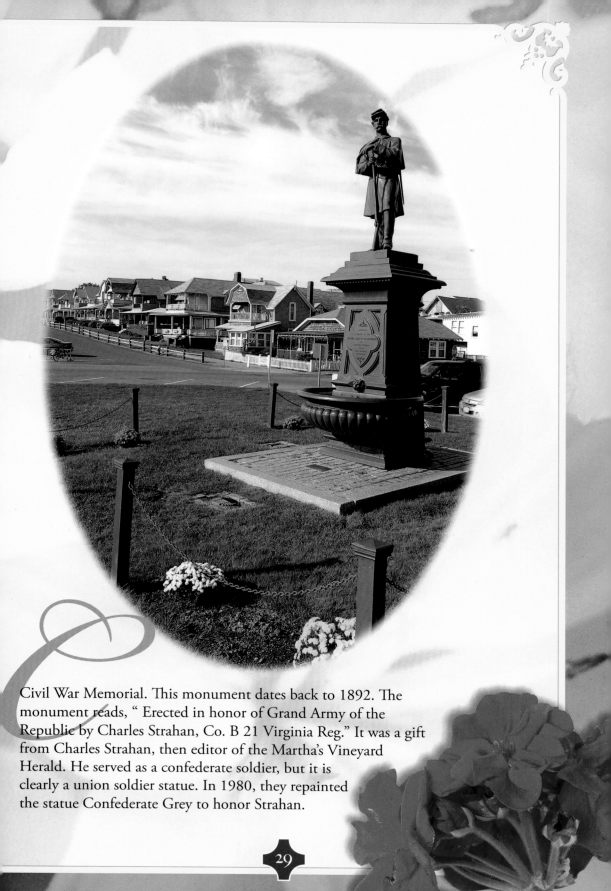

Civil War Memorial. This monument dates back to 1892. The monument reads, " Erected in honor of Grand Army of the Republic by Charles Strahan, Co. B 21 Virginia Reg." It was a gift from Charles Strahan, then editor of the Martha's Vineyard Herald. He served as a confederate soldier, but it is clearly a union soldier statue. In 1980, they repainted the statue Confederate Grey to honor Strahan.

Illumination Night. Illumination night marks the end of the summer season with the beautiful display of Japanese hanging lanterns and fireworks. This tradition dates back to over a century ago. They celebrate with song and open houses for friends and family. The event has become so popular that they do not announce the date until 1 week before the celebration.